Missing the Way

"They could not enter in."

How Israel missed God's rest

by

Patricia St John

Harvey Christian Publishers Inc.
449 Hackett Pike, Richmond, KY 40475
Email: books@harveycp.com
www.harveycp.com
Tel. 423 768 2297

CONTENTS

Chapter 1

Murmuring—The Sin of the People

From long experience and observation I am inclined to think that whoever finds redemption in the blood of Jesus has the choice of walking in the higher or the lower path. I believe the Holy Spirit at that time sets before him the more excellent way and incites him to walk therein, to choose the narrowest path in the narrowest way, to aspire after the heights and the depths of holiness—after the entire Image of God. But if he does not accept this offer, he insensibly declines into a lower order of Christians. He still goes on in what may be called a good way, serving God in his degree, and finds mercy at the end of life through the blood of the covenant.—John Wesley

The Book of Numbers is the record of a people to whom both roads were open, but they chose the lower one. God planned for them to enter into His rest. He had prepared for them a country, not where warfare should cease, but where warfare should be victorious and progressive; a country where all the promises of God would come true, where they would possess their possessions, and enjoy their inheritance; a country where hunger and thirst and aimless wandering would be a thing of the past. And they reached the very borders of it, and tasted the fruit of it, "But they could not enter into My rest."

Why? They desired it, and they weren't too bad.

The earlier chapters of the Book of Numbers give no record of any violent, gross sin, or murder, or immorality. It simply shows us the progress of a people who, while calling themselves the congregation of the Lord, indulged in seven "small," respectable sins—little, easily hidden sins that we indulge in daily, and gloss over, and explain away to ourselves and to other people. Yet each one proved an insuperable barrier to them when it came to entering into their inheritance, or even journeying towards it. All died within sight of the green hills and golden valleys; but they never possessed their possessions.

If these things are written for our example, it is vitally important that we should avoid the same pitfalls, lest we come to the end of our lives (and they race by so fast) hungry, thirsty, defeated, without ever having known the rest to which God has called us—the rest of a strenuous life of warfare with God, instead of battling against God; the rest of a life that accepts God's will gladly and rejoices in it, instead of continually rebelling and repining; the rest of a life that has ceased to fear and strive and compete for self, because self matters no longer; the rest of a life that habitually lays every burden on Jesus, and has therefore ceased to worry and fret.

And we who love Jesus, but know that we have not yet attained unto this rest, cry out with the writer to the Hebrews, "Let us therefore fear lest, a promise being left us of entering into His rest, any of us should seem to come short of it." Indeed, we fear desperately that we shall die without ever having entered in. "There remains a rest." We have seen it afar; we have read of it; we have sometimes tasted it; "But now, let us enter in."

"They could not enter in because of unbelief." But unbelief takes many ugly forms, and is the root of many poisonous fruits, and its first appearance in the Book of Numbers took the form of common-or-garden grumbling. "The people were complaining" (Numbers 11:1-3), and there was not, in this case, much to complain about—nothing specific—they were just fed up. It has been described as "a low chow-chow!" "Oh yes, we are all right; of course there's a lot to be thankful for, but...." That atmosphere of weary, depressed self-pity, that clouds our spiritual life, colors our conversation, and probably affects us physically. We begin to sag and drag, and to feel very tired indeed. People do not call it sin; they feel sorry for us, rather than blame us, and it is startling to notice that God classes murmuring with idolatry, fornication, and tempting the Lord.

"But the Lord heard," as well as the neighbors, and His anger was kindled. Besides, this general discontent had led on to a far more serious condition; they had now found a specific cause for their grumbling. The mixed multitude started it, those who had come out with them from Egypt, and had passed through the Red Sea. They were, however, not really God's people, and as far as we know they had never sat behind those closed doors, sheltered by the blood of the Passover lamb. Call them the nominal Christians, the church-attenders, brought up in Christian homes. They move along with the crowd but when it comes to that acid, individual test, "Are you content with Heaven's bread and nothing else?" they failed miserably. They remembered those things that the Egyptians enjoyed, the tasty food that had tickled their palates, and they forgot the whips and the taskmasters and the bondage. They lusted, and their influence spread to the very people of God.

"Nothing at all beside this manna"—that was the deep source of their discontent. At first they had enjoyed the manna immensely. It tasted like wafers made with honey and was quite a novelty, but they soon got tired of it. Their minds strayed back to the good old diet, and the more they savored it in imagination the more insipid the manna became.

They were no longer satisfied with what God provided. For us, this means Jesus, and He is all God ever promised us. He may add or take away a great many other mercies, but all we actually need to be content is in Jesus; and if He does not content us, nothing else ever will. When we long for the things this world can give, when we feel others have much and we have nothing, when life seems intolerably dull, we are, in fact, confessing that Christ has ceased to satisfy us. "Nothing at all," we mutter, "beside this manna!"

Blessed, blessed condition, no distractions! "Nothing at all," we say, and we can either spend our restless hungry days pining and complaining for those nothings, which would never have satisfied us in any case, or we can sit down and examine our assets. "Nothing…besides this manna"—then back to the manna! Can it satisfy us, or can it not? Did Jesus really mean anything when He said, "He that cometh to Me shall never hunger"?

"Oh," says the dissatisfied Christian, "I've tried it, but it doesn't work. The Bible seems insipid to me, and I can't concentrate in prayer." But the manna had to be gathered early, ground, beaten, and baked and eaten; it took time, patience, and hard work to be nourished by that bread. How much time have we spent daily with Jesus? How much mental energy and practical obedience have we given to Bible study? How serious and methodical has our prayer-life been? Don't call it off until you have tried fulfilling the conditions. He will be found of them that truly seek Him, but the seeking is costly, self-denying, disciplined work, and where we keep our part of the bargain, He will keep His. No one who ever sought Him with all their heart and mind and strength, giving to that search the time and purpose and energy and technical obedience that they would give to the supreme goal of their life, was ever disappointed. But those who treat that quest as a sideline, to be crowded in when possible and convenient, will always be disappointed.

"If any man thirst, let him come unto Me and drink," said Jesus, and the truly thirsty man desires nothing but water. Give him a bag of gold, and he will turn from it in disgust; he has diagnosed his own need and he wants water, and nothing but water. It is the complexity of our desires that prevents us from coming to Jesus. Far on in Christian service we thirst for recognition, for applause, for human encouragement and appreciation, for friendship, for success. We imagine they will satisfy us, and we keep one eye cocked toward them, and when we attain them they don't satisfy us at all. We have never learned that "our restless spirits yearn for Thee."

The saints have known it. David analyzed his own heart when he said, "One thing have I desired...that I might dwell in the house of the Lord." Augustine knew it when he said, "Thou hast made us for Thyself, and our hearts are restless until they find rest in Thee." But we do not know it. Like the man with the muck rake we look down to the dust instead of up to the glory. We are so sure some precious thing lies hidden in the dirt.

The mother was detained late, and the little children were becoming more tired and crosser every moment. Each wanted only what the other had, and having snatched it, discarded it with disgust within a few moments. Nothing pleased, and pandemonium reigned. The mother came at last and gathered the weary little creatures into her arms and listened to their stormy complaints: "I wanted that, and he wouldn't give it me," sobbed one. "And I wanted that, and he snatched it," wailed the other. "You both want your beds," said the mother gently, and in a few moments they were tucked in and asleep. She had analyzed their unrecognized desire for sleep, and firmly laid aside the toys to which they clung so wearily, and gathered them to their resting place.

Life is getting more and more complex. Beware lest the clutterings of our small wants and the grasping of little things make us blind to our great central thirst and desire of life. "Whom have I in Heaven but Thee, and there is none on earth that I desire beside Thee." Remember, too, that for all eternity we shall desire nothing else at all.

To be satisfied with Christ is to love His will, and to accept it gladly, whether He gives or withholds, and in acceptance lieth peace. "Good, perfect, acceptable will of God," cries the heart that knows and loves and has tasted that the Lord is gracious. Grumbling and complaining fall away, because in His will, gladly accepted, there is nothing to complain about. "I accept with both hands, and I praise," cries the soul that has entered into rest.

In Numbers 11:18-20 God gave the people what they wanted. They had plenty of meat at the end of the chapter, but they were sick and tired of it. He gave them their request, but sent leanness into their souls. And I repeat, because I believe it is the root of all our miseries and discontents and breakdowns, that if we are not satisfied with Jesus we shall never be satisfied with anything else. To desire Him, and to know that we desire Him only, is an ambition that will always satisfy, and for which we can strive all our lives, always achieving and always having more to achieve.

"We know as we follow on to know," each new beam of knowledge only showing us a new step of faith and obedience yet to be taken. We have set our faces to the sunlit heights of eternity, and ours is the patient joy of the mountaineer, who pauses on his little prominence so hardly won, and looks up to the immense, snowy heights above him. Unattainable? Perhaps. But he would die rather than turn back.

Chapter 2

Jealousy—The Sin of the Leaders

It was the sin of the high priest and the prophetess, the best and the highest in the land, the man and the woman who should have been closest to God. It is the sin that is probably inherent in us all, and the higher we rise, the more it tempts us. It is perhaps Satan's most potent secret weapon, crippling the lives of otherwise consecrated Christians far advanced in God's service—the sin of jealousy.

It is often difficult to recognize, because it has a subtle way of making us thoroughly muddled and inconsistent. What was really the root of the trouble in Numbers 12:1? Aaron could not really have been jealous of Moses' marriage, because he himself had made a far better one socially and politically, with the daughter of a prince of Judah. But a jealous person will seek any opportunity to disparage and discredit, and it was, perhaps, at that time, the only weakness in his brother that Aaron could criticize, and he made the very most of it.

It was an excuse, a handle, and in verse 2 the real reason of his jealousy bursts out: "Has God only spoken by Moses? Has He not also spoken by us?" In other words, "So-and-so is more blessed in his ministry than I, and I want to be thought as spiritual as he is. If I can somehow slightly discredit him, people may somehow think the better of me. If his voice could be heard a little less, perhaps mine would be heard a little more."

They forgot that it was not the voice of Moses to which men listened, but the voice of God, and the reason why God's words were heard so often and so clearly, was that Moses' words were heard so seldom. Moses was very meek, above all men on the face of the earth; so meek, so self-forgetful, so unconcerned about his own glory, that he had nothing to say about himself at all, and that was why God had a chance to speak. The lines were clear. God could transmit His messages without competition, and without Moses getting in the way. John the Baptist was in the same condition when he said, "I am a voice"...an instrument to be used by God to convey what message He chose. A voice means nothing, unless modified into reasonable words.

Miriam and Aaron wished to be voices conveying their own excellencies, and they probably succeeded for a time. No doubt many people listened to them. No doubt they sowed those seeds of jealousy and discontent which later sprung up as Korah's rebellion. No doubt they considerably undermined Moses' popularity and everybody heard about it; and then once again we have that telling little phrase, "and the Lord heard."

People may hear the hints we drop, the insinuations, the almost unnoticeable disparagements, the tone of our voice, the lack of praise, the silence that can be so damning, because "of course it wouldn't be right to criticize, but...." But the Lord heard the whole torrent of jealous exasperation and resentment, which probably never reached Aaron's lips, because after all, Aaron was a spiritual leader, and he would not want to be called a gossip or a tale-bearer. The Lord heard, and the Lord acted suddenly and swiftly.

Jealousy was the sin of the priest and the prophetess, and it is the sin of the pulpit, the pastorate, and the mission field. We recognize it as the devil's own weapon to cripple us spiritually; we hate it; we yearn to be free of it. It is a great day in our lives when God acts swiftly and suddenly, and shows us ourselves and blasts our insincerity and hypocrisy. "The Lord came down in a pillar of cloud" (v. 5), and poor, jealous Aaron was suddenly encircled with the glory of God, just as he had been on the first day of his appointment to the priesthood, when clothed in garments of glory and beauty, washed, crowned, and anointed, he had first lifted up his hands to bless the people.

Is it a shock, to stop sometimes in the middle of a day of hot, crowded, missionary routine, and to look back to the first high day of our consecration—perhaps those hours on board ship, when we re-dedicated ourselves to God for service? There we stood in the light of His Presence, and saw His glory:

Just as I am, young, strong, and free
To be the best that I can be.

How deeply sincere we were, but we have not always been the best, and perhaps we are no longer so young, or quite so strong. But God in His mercy descended again and restored the vision of His glory, and spoke again—not words of comfort, but words of judgment, like a skilful surgeon, who probes the cancer, and cuts it out remorselessly, that his patient may be restored to health.

First, God rebuked them sharply for their discontent and lack of trust. How dare they question God's dealings with another? Then comes that solemn question, "Were you not afraid to speak against My servant?" No, we have not always been afraid. We have criticized right and left. We forget God's law, "Go, tell thy brother his fault between thee and him alone." We have disparaging little chats with fellow-Christians who have only heard our side, and who sympathetically agree that so-and-so is really very trying indeed.

Then the glory of the Lord departed, and there stood Miriam, white with leprosy, the outward sign of her inward corruption. Both suddenly saw themselves, and realized not only from whence, but to where, they had fallen. Perhaps Aaron had been deceived by the beauty of his robes, and the honor of his office, and had forgotten that, apart from the sacrifice, he was a sinner in filthy garments. Missionaries and preachers have a high reputation, and we can cover up our inward corruption for a long time. But it is a great day in our lives when the glory of the Lord comes down, and we gaze at Jesus and turn back and gaze at ourselves, and see, in the lingering light of His love and character, the mixed motives, the self-deception, the jealousies. It is a great day when others see them too, because then we can never pretend again. "Dead...powerless for God." "Half-consumed...corrupt and infectious."

Miriam was cast on the prayers of the one of whom she was so jealous, and so for a long, quiet week she went without the camp. "Let us therefore go forth unto Him without the camp, bearing His reproach" (Heb. 13:14). Jesus is always waiting outside the camp. That is where the world put Him, because they thought nothing of Him, and that is where He has waited to meet us ever since. Set free at last from the bondage of competing with another, from the strain of keeping up her reputation, shunned of all because of her obvious corruption, she found One Who would accept her as she was. At the cross we are welcome, leprosy and all, and it is only there, with no eyes upon us save the eyes of Jesus that we shall ever find rest.

"The labor of self-love is a heavy one indeed," wrote a recent writer. "The heart's efforts to protect itself, and to shield its touchy honor from men's opinions, will never let the heart have rest. Yet man carries the burden continually, cringing under criticism, smarting under slights, tossing sleepless if another is preferred before them. Jesus calls us to rest, and meekness is His method. The meek man cares not who is greater than he, for he has long ago decided that the world's esteem is not worth the effort. He has accepted God's estimate of his own life, and he knows himself as weak as God has declared him to be, but in the sight of God of more importance than angels; so he rests content, and allows God to place His own values. The old struggle to defend himself is over.

"To all victims of this gnawing disease of pride, jealousy, pretence, Jesus says, 'become as little children,' for little children do not compare. They enjoy what they have without relating it to what others have. Only as they grow older does the burden of jealousy come down on them, and it never leaves them until Jesus sets them free. Artificiality drops away the moment we kneel at the feet of Jesus and surrender to His meekness. Then what we are will be everything; what we appear will no longer matter."

So without the camp Miriam found rest and healing, and came back. We do not hear of her again, except that she lived and died with the people of God, but we know that Aaron's position was revindicated and his rod budded. His spiritual authority was restored when his jealousy was dealt with, and he lived and died as God's high priest.

Chapter 3

Unbelief—The Sin of the People

And Moses said, Get you up...go up into the mountain, and see the land, what it is...and bring of the fruit of the land (Num. 13:17-20).

The great moment had arrived; the climax toward which they had been traveling and for which they had been hoping from the hour they left Egypt. The call came on an ordinary day of desert routine. "Get you up, go up into the mountain, further and higher than you've been before. See the land; view the prospects of really believing in God and of total obedience; weigh it up! Is it too hard? What will you gain? What will you lose? Is it too expensive? Bring of the fruits. Is the Spirit-filled life really practical?"

So the spies went forward to prospect and came back with their majority vote: "It is not for us; the difficulties are too great. Far better settle down where we are and forget about it" (verses 27-29). In other words, we might paraphrase their attitude in more modern speech: "The life of faith and obedience and victory is all very well for so-and-so, but it is not for me. My nature is too difficult, my circumstances too crippling, my companions too trying. I am too bogged down by my past. Our enemies are stronger than we are and we cannot overcome."

They took the first step that leads to victory, but they never took the second. "We were in our own sight as grasshoppers" (v. 33), they said, and to feel a grasshopper, to know that "without

Him I can do nothing," is a necessary stage in our own progress, but we must never settle down there. In Christian circles, our false humility, our diffidence, shyness, and timidity may pass as virtue and men may call it humility and praise it. But God has a different name for it. "They could not enter in," explains the writer of the Hebrews, "because of their unbelief."

We find that unbelief begets depression, another respectable sin (read 14:1). They sat down and wept all night and their depression (verses 3 and 4) killed faith, hope, and reason, as it does nowadays. At such times we echo their words: "Has it really paid being a Christian?" "It is not only me who is suffering, but I'm worried about my family. We all managed much better before we obeyed God. This place of service to which He called me is so difficult, that I feel I must pull out and go elsewhere. Victory in these circumstances is not for me."

The lonely voices may have made them hesitate. "The land is good," cried Joshua and Caleb; "don't rebel against God… don't fear the people" (verses 6-9). Inaction resulting from fear is rebellion against God. God says, "Go, do, speak," and we say, "I can't, I'm too scared, or too shy, or too depressed." There are a few clear, battle-cry voices urging us on and we know in our hearts that this is the voice of God, but the pessimists and our own fearful hearts tell us that it would be most unwise and risky. Stay in the rut where you are," they say; "at least it is safe and respectable."

It applies to geographical ventures and spiritual ventures. There come times in our lives at home, and on the mission field, when we are confronted by a situation that overwhelms us. It may be a wrong relationship and the voice of the Spirit cries out with clarion clearness, "Get you up, put it right; humble yourself; confess your sin. Rise up at all costs, to love, atone, and overcome evil with good." But we cringe in our corners: "I just could not face him. It would be too humiliating; I have been too hurt. I am too afraid of rebuffs. It is better to creep away from the situation, and let things be." So we sit and think about it, turning over our vain regrets, brooding instead of acting, while depression comes down on us like a black cloud which blots out the face of God. We are left alone with our impotent selves... wounded grasshoppers.

Perhaps we have failed and made mistakes in a certain situation. The way is still open to go back, try again, and put it right, but our self-confidence has been badly shaken, and we are too depressed or ashamed to learn from our mistakes. We cannot get up. It is easier to slide back, to withdraw completely, or simply to crawl on in the same surroundings, too shy and diffident to be of any further use, hiding our talents, repressing our personalities, withholding through false modesty what we might contribute—useful in a degree, but never again the man or woman God meant us to be.

Or there is a door of opportunity open to us, a call to advance. But it requires a tremendous effort, and it doesn't seem very prudent. We are perhaps middle-aged by now, wedded to our comfortable routine, mental sloth, caution, love of physical ease. The warning voices of our kind friends hold us back. ("My dear, it would be far too much for you; it couldn't be expected at your age; think what it might lead to...I shouldn't dream of getting involved.") And we do think, and we decide not to get involved, and the voice of God's trumpet dies away. We simply could not face the change. "It would have been far too much for me," we say. "It would not have been fair on my family." And everyone is most sympathetic: "My dear," they say, "I'm sure you were perfectly right.

From prayer that asks that I may be
Sheltered from winds that beat on Thee,
From faltering when I should aspire,
From sinking, when I should climb higher,
From silken self, Oh Captain, free
Thy soldier who would follow Thee.
From subtle love of softening things,
From easy choices, weakenings,
Not thus are spirits fortified,
Not this way went the Crucified.
From all that dims Thy Calvary,
Oh, Lamb of God, deliver me.

—Amy Carmichael

The voices of our friends must often dim His Calvary, and God's assessment of the situation was very different. "How long will it be ere they believe Me?" (Numbers 14:11). How often He might say it of us: "Have all their personal experiences of My saving grace and provision, all the teaching they have had, all the meetings they have attended, all the hymns they have sung, never taught them to believe in Me?" "Where my Savior leads I'll follow," we trill happily, gathered in a warm, bright room round a piano with our fellow-Christians. Does that vow mean anything when we stand at the doors of the Promised Land alone with Jesus?

Or perhaps we have simply lost hope. We have been brought up on the best Keswick lines, and we know all about the doctrine of dying to self and victory over sin. We may even know Romans 6 by heart; we could give you the formula every time, but it just hasn't worked, and now, well on in life, we feel pretty sure that it never will. We are afraid to apply the formula again, because it is too disappointing. In a day or two we shall crash again, as we have always done in the past, and, we add in the recesses of our unbelieving souls, as we always shall do. So we settle down to end our days in the wilderness, but the vision of what might have been never quite leaves us. Thank God, our hearts will always be restless until they find rest in Him.

Let us, for the moment, forget all about the formula and look at those simple words of Caleb's and Joshua's: "Let us go up at once...the Lord will bring us in...the Lord is with us" (Num. 13:30). Maybe we cannot trust the teaching any longer, but perhaps we can still trust the Lord. "Go up at once," said Caleb. Don't sit down and imagine the defeat that might come tomorrow, or the enormous size of the enemies we may meet in two days' time, or the bitter disappointments we shall have undergone in a week's time. Get up at once, put on your armor and start to walk up the hill with God; just take the next immediate step of present obedience with Jesus, and when you have done it, take the next step, still trusting in Jesus. It is not His way to show you the second step until you have taken the first, and we often fail because we try to look ahead instead of following Him. The next step is always plain, and Jesus is always there, and it is always in present action that His victory is experienced, never in future imagination. The devil will do his best to fill the future with terror for anyone who is foolish enough to be intimidated by him, but it is only now, at this present moment of obedience, that the grace and power of God are to be found. "We have nothing to do with life in the aggregate," wrote an old divine. "Each moment brings its duties, responsibilities, and needs. Our business is to live a moment at a time, and that moment for God. Think not on a holy life, but on a holy moment as it flies."

A well-known Bible teacher was crossing the Atlantic and was asked to lead Bible readings for the passengers. One bright moonlight night he strolled out on deck and was accosted by a lady sitting in a deck-chair. "Dr. S," she said, "I cannot agree with your teaching. That life of holiness you described this afternoon is surely only for the special few, not for the ordinary Christian." The doctor sat down a short distance away from her. "It's a beautiful moonlight night," he remarked. "Yes," she replied, rather disappointed at such an abrupt turn of the subject.

"Look at that track of moonlight over the sea," said the doctor. "It is coming right to my feet." "On the contrary," smiled the lady, "it appears to be coming right to mine." "It is coming to mine, to yours, and to the feet of everyone who looks at the moon," replied the doctor. "And when Jesus walked this earth, He left a single track of radiant holiness for us to follow, and that track is not for the chosen few. It comes straight to the feet of every repentant sinner who looks to Jesus."

And so it is; the water on either side may seem very black and stormy, but the track leads straight to Jesus; not to complication or involvement or disappointment—these are only incidental. The Israelites thought they were being led to the bitterness of Marah, the thirst of Rephidim, the drought and hunger of Sinai, but God's summary of that journey was different. "I brought you unto Myself," He said (Exodus 19:4). Jesus Himself is the end and goal of every faltering step of faith and obedience. "Where will this lead me?" we cry, and the answer is, "It will lead me to Jesus."

They could not believe that God would carry them through. Later on they repented, but the moment for action had passed. Unbelief was forgiven, but life was never what it might have been. But, thank God, the goal of our pilgrimage is no tract of land. The material opportunity may pass by, leaving us with lifelong regrets but, thank God, the call to enter God's promised land of rest will last as long as life lasts. Sometimes, only through the wilderness of our lost opportunities and self-despair do we grope our way to true belief—the belief that will cause us to rise up, conquer the mountain, and enter the land.

Chapter 4

Pride—The Sin of the Levites

The earlier part of the Book of Numbers seems to spotlight the Levites, and the subject of their calling and appointment keeps recurring. In 1 Chronicles 23:24-28, we are told that they were to do the service of the House of the Lord, and to wait on the sons of Aaron. It was not a top job, and there seems to have been no hope of promotion. They had to fetch and carry and understudy for those directly employed in the priesthood, and to stand at special times to praise, and sacrifice, and pray.

We are told they were not to be numbered for war (Num. 1:48-9). Because of their specialized work for the House of God, they were to be set free from the ordinary, secular duties of daily life. They were what you might call the full-timers in God's service, and in Num. 1:50 and 4:15 a telling little glimpse is given of what that service involved—"they shall bear"—and a certain section of the Levites had to bear even heavier burdens than the rest. The Levites were given wagons, "but unto the sons of Kohath he gave none, because the service of the sanctuary that belonged unto them was that they should bear upon their shoulders (Num. 7:9). To them belonged the tremendous and priceless responsibility of bearing the ark, although they never actually saw what they carried. To the priest belonged the glory of handling and packing up that precious casket, and gazing on the bloodstain. To the sons of Kohath belonged the hot march, the bowed, aching shoulders, tramping along through the scorching desert sand while others relaxed in vehicles. There was no glamour, and no easing up…just sheer hard work, harder than anyone else's.

In Numbers 3:45-51 we find the Levites were to be numbered, but not for war. Each was to represent before God the redemption of an Israelite. They stood responsible to God for the spiritual life of another, and therefore, because of that tremendous responsibility, God said, "The Levites shall be Mine" (3:12), "clean" (8:17), "separated" (8:14), "wholly given unto Me" (8:16).

Lastly, they were to have no inheritance (18:20). They could never settle down. Everyone else had their own secure homestead, but the Levites were forever spiritual strangers and pilgrims. The Lord was their Inheritance, and they were asked to be content with that and to live a life of praise.

Servants to someone in a higher position than themselves, doing the routine jobs that no one would praise them for, punctually keeping those hours of praise and prayer throughout the nights when everyone else was asleep and no one was watching save God; being, rather than doing; working harder, having less rest and ease than the others, without the comfort and security of an inheritance—unless fully conscious of the intrinsic honor and glory of His calling and in love with His true Inheritance, the Levite would have had every reason to be discontented. Judging by material values, he was the worst off every time, and the whole glory of his calling seems to have been to do without.

But some of these sons of Kohath got into bad company (Num. 16:1) and began to listen to critical, discontented talk, talk that stung their pride, and resulted in the following kind of thinking: "So-and-so is too big for his boots. Why him, and not me? ...I'm just as capable of leadership as he is; am I going on in this rut all my life: How about a spot of promotion...a bigger, more showy position? In short, God made me a Levite, but I should prefer to be a priest. He separated me, appointed me, ordained me to a special work, but it doesn't quite satisfy my ego. I want something more spiritually important."

"Spiritually important"—the words are a contradiction; we can become more socially important, more academically important by honest hard work, by push, by self-effort, by initiative, by competition, but, in a sense, we can only become more spiritually important by becoming less important. Korah had never been less "spiritually important" in his life than on that day when he stood before Moses and said, in effect, "I'm as good as Aaron, and I want a more spiritual job." In fact, he had ceased to be of any spiritual importance at all. Through listening to foolish, worldly talk, he had made the pitiful mistake of thinking that to wear a mitre and a crown and to stand in a prominent place and bless the people would somehow make him a greater man of God. He had completely lost sight of that great, basic principle of service, that my spiritual importance and stature is measured by what I am, never by what I do, or say, or wear, still less by what anyone else thinks or says about me.

Spiritual pride blinds our spiritual understanding and discernment, and Moses turned and spoke to Korah alone, the man who had known God; he had nothing to say, just then, to the sons of Reuben.

"Seemeth it a small thing unto you that the God of Israel hath separated you...to bring you near unto Himself to do the service of the tabernacle of the Lord, and to stand before the congregation to minister unto them?" (v. 9). In other words, he said, "Has your spiritual pride blinded you to your amazing present opportunities? By longing for something more important and showy, have you overlooked and neglected the service God actually gave you? Have you missed the glory and duty of working for God today in the place where He put you?" It is in that duty, in that sphere, that all grace, all supply, all spiritual sufficiency is to be found, and it is there that, today, I have the opportunity of knowing God, and serving Him, and drawing near to Him, and is that a small thing? It is for that task, and not for another, that He will fill me with His Holy Spirit; it is just there, in the routine position, doing those dull jobs, meeting that same old set of uninteresting people, that He has promised His blessing. Don't despise these circumstances, because they are the medium through which God purposes to make Himself known to you, and be very, very sure of His leading before you seek to change them.

Spiritual pride also blinded his eyes to God's requirements. He must have really thought that God would accept his incense offered in pride and anger and self-vindication, or he would never have dared bring it. Even Dathan and Abiram had more sense than that! By what tortuous process of thought he mentally justified himself, we do not know; his reason and self-knowledge were clouded by his pride. Apart from the continual light of God's judgment on our life, we can justify almost anything we please. "See if there be any wicked way in me," cried David, because apart from God's searchlight, I cannot always see it myself.

What a ghastly moment of self-revelation there must have been, when God's glory suddenly shone on them, not in mercy now but in judgment. It had been there all the time; it was the same glory in the light of which Korah had been chosen to walk daily, the glory that should have transfigured his daily toil, lightened his load, and made him the happiest man on earth. But the light that would guide us, cheer us, and warm our hearts, becomes, if refused, the light of judgment. We cannot escape, one way or another. The glory will never be dimmed.

So the earth swallowed them up, because the service of spiritual pride is neither acceptable to God or man. Heaven refuses it, and earth rejects it. The whole tainted family of Dathan and Abiram disappeared, but we read that the sons of Korah died not. God judges and purifies His chosen people, but He does not annihilate them. Purged of their pride and recommissioned (Num. 18:2), content to accept the limitations God had imposed on them (18:3), realizing their inheritance, they became the sweetest singers in Israel, for no one sings so sweetly as he who has been redeemed from death. The burden of their song was this: "This Lord is the portion of my inheritance and of my cup. Thou maintainest my lot. The lines are fallen unto me in pleasant places; yea, I have a goodly heritage...I had rather be a doorkeeper in the house of my God than to dwell in the tents of wickedness....No good thing will He withhold from them that walk uprightly."

Chapter 5

Spiritual Depression—The Sin of the Leader

No one would have blamed Moses nowadays if he had collapsed with a full-scale nervous breakdown. The whole project seemed hopeless. He was single-handed, desperately overworked, involved in a situation that was not even originally of his own choosing, frustrated at every step, actively opposed, criticized, misunderstood, threatened by the very people for whom he was wearing himself out. Physically, no doubt, the climate and the constant traveling had taken it out of him, and now there was this new complication of discontent and grumbling over the diet.

He was suffering badly from physical and mental exhaustion and nervous frustration. Had he lived nowadays, he would have been advised to visit his psychiatrist, take a tonic, improve his diet, knock off work completely, and relax in different surroundings. But none of these prescriptions were available or practical in the wilderness of Sinai, so Moses had either to succumb to his condition and let go, or else find some other remedy. And the wonderful part of the story is, that, right there in the wilderness, with the pressure increased instead of lightened, and no change of his physical circumstances—except for the worse—Moses found mental and spiritual healing.

Unfortunately, the details of his treatment are not recorded, except that some practical help was given in the organization of the camp; but this would not really have lightened the spiritual strain or the mental frustration. The man who had cried, "I am not able to bear all this people alone, because it is too heavy for me," still had to bear alone the unreasonable jealousy of his own brother and sister, the anxiety of Miriam's illness, the crushing disappointment of the report of the ten spies, the people's reaction, the defeat of the two, and the final rebellion and fear of stoning. And in Numbers 14 the man who had broken down (ch. 11) stands again before God under far greater pressure and temptation—the man whose whole life-work has apparently failed and fallen into dust and ashes before him. And yet this time, Moses did not break down.

Three tremendous temptations must have been present with Moses as he listened to the voice of God (ch. 14), as though God Himself was testing him when the fire was hottest, and when, humanly speaking, he had more excuse to fail than ever before. The first was simply the temptation to his tired body to give it all up. God put it to him: "How long will this people provoke Me?...I will smite them."

His weary body and strained mind must have grasped at it! "Just drop it all; lay down the responsibility for ever...it is possible now. God has offered you this way out. You said before, 'I am not able to bear it,' and now you need not bear it. Go on alone to the Promised Land, and rest and enjoy the milk and honey." But somehow, through some process unrecorded, Moses' attitude had changed. He conquered this temptation because he had come to understand the power of God. Instead of crying, "Have I conceived, that Thou shouldst say, 'Carry them in thy bosom'?" he has learned to cast the weight back on the bosom of the Father. "Thou broughtest up this people...Thou goest before them."

All those who accept Christian leadership must share to a certain extent the burden that Christ bears. But it is His burden that He shares with us, not ours that we share with Him. Like St. Christopher, who in the legend undertook to carry the Christ Child across the river, there are times when we feel that we are sinking. But the strength that the saint needed to keep his footing, somehow flowed from the very weight that was bowing him down.

Helpless I floundered—all my strength
  Succumbed beneath the increasing load;
I failed; yet failing, still stood firm.
  For radiant from the Child there flowed,
Not weight alone, but strength to bear
  Pain, and the courage to endure.
Love to fulfill all love's demands,
  One the affliction with the cure. . . .
He bows me down; He holds me up.
  Through sucking mud, and clinging weed,
For I am weak, and He is strong,
  His sustenance supplies my need.
Oh, bitter toil! Oh, perfect rest!
  Oh, starlight on the troubled sea!
I place my yielded hands in His;
  The child I carry, beareth me.

A tiny child was staggering along, lugging a basket of groceries far too heavy for it. All offers of help had been firmly refused, but his small aching arms could manage no longer. Suddenly a way dawned on him: "Mummy," he called to the mother who was only waiting to take over, "I know what we'll do; I'll carry the basket, and you carry me!" Previously, Moses had looked at the demands made on him; now he looked at the source of supply; before he had measured the weight of the burden; now he was calculating the strength of the everlasting arms. His cry is no longer "The burden is too heavy," but, "For Thy glory, let us go on bearing this burden together."

The second temptation would have been strong at that moment to a lesser man than Moses: "Let God do as He suggests, and send a pestilence, and you can get your revenge without having to lift a finger. Let God pay them back for all the threats and disloyalty, the hatred and ingratitude. As, a short time ago, they lifted up their hands to stone you, so let God stretch forth His hand and avenge your wrongs." Yet Moses had not, apparently, the slightest wish to have his wrongs avenged. Earlier on, how gladly would he have been rid of them at any cost, but now he has come to understand, even to share, the character of God. He pleads that character, and in doing so, clothes himself with its attributes. "The Lord is long-suffering, of great mercy, forgiving iniquity and transgression…pardon, I beseech Thee, the iniquity of this people, as Thou hast forgiven from Egypt until now."

Paul prayed that the Ephesians would be able to understand the length of the love of Christ, and this can probably only be done by contemplating Christ Himself and the length to which His love went. It went infinitely far beyond our reach and comprehension, but united to Christ we are carried forward, as a sluggish drop of water, dropped into a swift, bright current, is merged with the stream and carried toward the sea.

The third test implied getting something for himself out of the situation: "I will make of thee a great nation." In other words, "Take the glory to yourself, and the land for your own children." Worldly ease, popularity, and earthly glory lay within his grasp, as it lay at the feet of the Lord Jesus when He stood on the high mountain and gazed at the kingdoms of this world spread out in front of Him. The pride and glory of life was with easy reach, but Moses had learned the supreme value of the glory of God, and nothing else mattered to him now. "The Egyptians will hear of it," he cried. "The nations will say, The Lord was not able to bring this people into the land." The reputation of God's power and glory was at stake, and Moses never gave a thought to his own glory.

"The Holy Ghost was not yet given because Jesus was not yet glorified." The surface meaning of these words is obvious, but perhaps there is also a deeper hidden meaning. When we cry out for the fullness of the Holy Spirit, for a deeper knowledge of God, for His power in service, what are the true motives of our beseeching? What am I really asking? Is it that I may be more successful in my Christian life, that I may achieve more, and be more admired in the Christian world? Or is it that Christ may be glorified? God will only bestow His power on us for one reason, and that is for His own glory. "Power is a dangerous weapon, and our God is a jealous God," wrote Paget Wilkes of Japan; "He will not give it to anyone who is not entirely sanctified." Many of us probably know with sorrow that our motives are mixed, but Moses was single minded, and the importance of the glory of God had flooded out all his self-seeking. "Nothing for me; all for Thee," is a prayer irresistible to God. It is true prayer in His Name, and according to His will, and nothing can be denied it. Clear and strong comes the eternal answer in verses 20 and 21: "I have pardoned according to thy word, but as truly as I live, all the earth shall be filled with the glory of the Lord."

If that is really what we want, that others shall be pardoned and that God shall be glorified, we may be sure that we shall get it, whatever that prayer involves of anguish and self-denial in the process of its fulfillment. There is no fear of breaking down through frustration and disappointment, because it asks nothing for itself, and if you expect nothing you cannot be disappointed. The old monk expressed this attitude in his short prayer: "Give me—to God, a heart of flame; to others, a heart of love; to myself a heart of steel."

No! There was no need for Moses to break down. The remedy was close at hand: The power of God, the refuge to which he fled with all his feelings of insecurity and inadequacy, and found it sufficient; the character of God, longsuffering, gentle, merciful and loving, with which he could clothe himself as with an armor, and find it proof against jealousy, anger, resentment, and the desire to revenge; and finally, the glory of God, the single motive that kept his feet on course, and forged him into an integrated personality with a single undeviating purpose, to further that glory. The remedy was as close to him in the Sinai desert as it is to us today, amidst the frustrations and strain of the mission field, or the hectic pace and competition of modern business life; in our tensions and wrong relationships, and our fears of the future. Let us try it out first of all, and perhaps we shall not need to resort to the other remedies. Perhaps, instead, we shall be able to make these songs of victory our own, "Thou hast delivered my soul from death, my eyes from tears, and my feet from falling. I will walk (not break down) before the Lord, in the land of the living."

> *My soul, thou hast proved thy God;*
> *And canst thou fear now?*
> *Behold Him, thy Light and thy Cover.*
> *Thy Champion, Companion and Lover.*
> *Thy Stay when the foeman oppresses,*
> *Thy song 'midst a thousand distresses.*

Chapter 6

Impatience—The Sin of the Leaders

"Wherefore have ye made us come out of Egypt to bring us into this evil place?" cried the people. This "evil place" was Kadesh, north of the desert, near the borders of the Promised Land, and these people spoke an everlasting truth. There is no place so thirsty and dreary as the borders of the land—we have come so far, we have sacrificed so much, we have hoped so greatly. We have seen the fruit, and talked to those whose feet have been over the borders, but we have never entered in. The worldling who never set out from Egypt, or those who may have turned back early on the march, have their own satisfactions. They have never known anything else, and the leeks, and onions, and garlics are all they want. But the soul on the borders is haunted by an eternal restlessness that nothing can satisfy.

These were the people Moses had to deal with, and it was not his fault that they were so unhappy. He had done his best under God to lead them in; the refusal had been theirs, and now day after day he was left to deal with them and their thoroughly disappointing behavior. And now this new spate of faithless grumbling, and blaming the leaders for circumstances quite beyond their control....Were they God's people or were they not? So much depends on the answer. In every movement of God there are hangers-on and the rice-Christians. Every true building produces a mass of rubbish. There are always tares among the wheat, but Christ's injunction to the reapers was, "Let the tares grow with the wheat." The wood, the hay, and the stubble will be burned with fire at the judgment seat, but until then it seems that they have a part to play in the perfecting of the Church.

There were times in the desert when God stretched out His hand and cleared away the rubbish in one fell swoop, by earthquake, sword, or fiery serpent, but He never entrusted this work to Moses; He always did it Himself. As far as Moses was concerned, this motley, irritating crowd of discontented people was God's congregation, entrusted to his loving care. These were the people whom God had fed with manna, and whom He intended to satisfy with water from the rock. Many of them would lift dying eyes to the brazen serpent, and find new life in the very near future, and journey on singing toward the sunrising, and cause wells to spring up with praise. Yes, God still counted them His people, and was willing to forgive and lead them on as far as they would go; Moses gave up too soon.

It was one of those critical times when the glory of the Lord had appeared to Moses and he had gazed for a moment on the character of God—patient, longsuffering, and of great mercy—and as we who have seen the glory of God shining in the face of Jesus Christ have no excuse to misrepresent Him to men, so Moses had seen the pattern, and the character he had been called to bear. He was to gather the thirsty congregation together, lead them to a cliff nearby, and speak to it, and the water would flow out.

Years before, in Horeb, at the outset of their journey, he had smitten a large boulder, but Christ the Rock, smitten in death, will never be smitten again. The smitten rock has become the sheltering cliff—the shade from the heat, the refuge in time of storm, Christ risen and exalted, our source of supply and our shelter. It was to this cliff that Moses was told to bring his worthless, troublesome, failing congregation, and to come back and back and back in patient faith and hope and love, claiming the living waters for himself and for them—the water that would refresh them, and lift up their heads, and cause them to travel onwards, and the power of claiming it had been given to Moses: "Speak to the rock."

I am an empty vessel, not one thought
Or look of love I ever to Thee brought;
But I can come and come again to Thee,
With this, the empty sinner's only plea,
Thou lovest me.

How did Moses fail? Listen to his words, "Hear now, ye rebels!" Hope had died. To him they were no longer the people of God, redeemed by the blood of the Lamb, and therefore infinitely precious. He saw them now simply from a human standpoint, a band of rebels. He forgot the price of their redemption, and therefore considered them worthless and hopeless, and there are always the two standpoints, "the weak brother" or "the brother for whom Christ died." My weak brother may seem a hopeless case to me, and not worth bothering about, but, whether I like it or not, the brother for whom Christ died will be held and perfected to eternity.

Until, made beautiful by love divine,
He in the likeness of his Lord shall shine,
and in casting him off I am only estranging myself from my Redeemer and his.

On my shelf stands a dirty little clay lampstand, small and dingy but perfect. It was dug up in the ruins of Tyre, and years ago I stood on that historic shore where the fishermen spread out their nets on the ancient foundations, and someone handed it to me. Ardent spring-cleaners threaten to throw it away; children pounce on it as a plaything. If a dealer in antiques came along, he might offer me a price for it, but I shall never sell it. I guard it from the lot of them, because finding that little lampstand was one of the great experiences of my life. The child and the spring-cleaner may rightly claim that the clay is not worth a farthing, but I see the touch of the hand of a craftsman who may have sat with the prophets and patriarchs, and to me it is priceless—a link with the eternal centuries. So there are always the two assessments: the things that are seen that are temporal. And the things that are not seen that are eternal.

"Must I fetch you water out of this rock?" went on Moses; love had died. He no longer desired their salvation. It had become a tedious duty to satisfy them and lead them to the rock. In a fit of impatient ill-temper, he hit out at the face of the cliff. No grateful joy surged up within him when he saw their thirst slaked and the grumbling turned to praise. He was fed up with them, and they could sink or swim for all he cared just then.

And so for one act of bad temper and impatience, Moses and Aaron lost the goal of their journey, and the ambition of their life, and on first thoughts, our judgment rebels at the severity of their punishment; it seems out of proportion to the crime. But if these things are written for our learning, then they illustrate an eternal principle, that we cannot make spiritual progress alone.

Down to Gehenna or up to the throne,
He travels fastest who travels alone,

may be true in many realms, but not in the spiritual. The links are horizontal as well as vertical, and Moses himself was one of God's congregation and he could not detach himself. Every step forward he made toward God must be made bowed under the burden of their welfare. The shepherd could not come home alone; that would have been too easy. He must struggle up the hillside with the sheep on his shoulders. Christ would not return to glory until He could enter in with those sublime words on His lips, "Behold I, and the children whom God has given Me." So keep on, and don't give up until God gives up.

So Moses' life was blasted, and all the years of suffering and travail wasted because of one act of impatience and bad temper? Not at all! God's goal for Moses was not to set his feet on any particular tract of land, but to lead him further and further in the way of holiness, and from now onwards Moses had to scale spiritual heights he had never known before. He had to go back to where had had failed and lead on the same set of people to enter the land without him. Without bitterness, or jealousy, or resentment he had to start to prepare a younger man to succeed where he had failed. And he did it! In the sight of his own people, disinherited and rejected; in the sight of God, a mighty victor in his selflessness, humility, and the quiet acceptance of God's will

And did he never reach the goal of his life? Of course he did. Years later, Christ stood in white shining raiment on a pinnacle of the Promised Land, looking out over the length and breadth of it, and Moses came and stood beside Him. He was there at last, but as far as we know, he did not look much at the fruitful hills and valleys, because he was looking at Christ, and talking of His death; every prayer Moses had ever prayed was answered, all his desires were fulfilled, and all his heartaches and regrets were healed and forgotten.

Are you seeking to achieve some tremendous goal? Have you some worthy aim to which you have given your strength, your love, and your very life? Do you sometimes fear that at the end it will all be a failure? Then take your eyes off that goal and turn them to Christ. He may, or may not, give you the thing that you are aiming for, but He will give you all that you truly, deeply want, and satisfy every unfulfilled desire, and in Him there is no failure, no falling short. Up there we shall find all our right aims completed and achieved in Him, and to know Him is to enter into rest.

Chapter 7

The Remedy

NUMBERS 21

"The People were much discouraged because of the way," and one might ask, "What was wrong with the way?" The trouble was, they had been there so often before. It was the same old Red Sea they had crossed in such triumph years ago, the same old Mount Hor, where they had made such high vows and resolves. It was all so near and yet so far, and anyhow, what had it all come to? Here they were in the same old thirsty desert, fed up with the same old manna, kowtowing to the same old Moses—no progress, no apparent fulfillment of promises, stagnation and defeat, facing, and failing the same old temptations. We have all known the feeling in our own hearts:

> *It is not finished, Lord;*
> *There is not one thing done.*
> *There is no battle in my life,*
> *That I have really won.*
> *And now I come to tell Thee,*
> *How I strive and fail,*
> *The human, all too human tale,*
> *Of weakness and futility.*
> —Studdert Kennedy.

But what years of wasted life it takes us to see the truth! Instead of blaming themselves, they all got together to blame something or someone else. God, Whose promise had failed ("Christianity does not work, it has not come up to my expectations, and one has to be realistic"); Moses, the leader ("They are such stick-in-the-muds! If we had an able, modern, go-ahead leader, who would listen to us, something might happen!"); the wilderness around them ("My circumstances are impossible. It is just not practical to live the Christian life in my environment"); the manna ("The Bible means nothing to me; it just doesn't get across, so I've stopped reading it").

Once again, God acted drastically, and sent fiery serpents among the people, and many died, and within five minutes of that bite, everybody was perfectly clear where the trouble lay, and no one was looking round, or blaming God, or the manna, or Moses, or the desert any more. Every man's eyes were on himself, and his own desperate, immediate need of healing. To refuse to face the trouble or the remedy now would be swift death. This terrible tragedy became their greatest blessing—their only hope of life. It turned their eyes straight in on their poisoned selves, and straight out in desperate hope on Jesus. The crisis was so sharp that it no longer helped to blame anyone or anything else. The drama must now be acted out between the dying sinner and the ready Savior, all else forgotten, and when we come to this point something always happens. If God cannot win us, and turn our eyes on Himself except by open crushing disaster, then open crushing disaster will fall; He loves us too much to withhold it. If we will only look and live from the jaws of death, then He will bring us to the jaws of death, that He might raise us up again, and the valley of weeping becomes a well, and the Valley of Achor, a door of Hope.

There were the same old temptations, and in verse 7 there are the same old words they had said before: "We have sinned." But this time there was a difference. They had reached a crisis in their lives, and God revealed to them a truth they had never grasped before. The Lord said, "Make thee a brazen serpent, and put it on a pole, and it shall come to pass, that everyone that is bitten, when he looketh upon it, shall live." Every man who crawled to the door of his tent and lifted dying eyes to that emblem would appropriate it to himself; "that is the serpent that bit me; that is the source of the poison and pain and fever racking my body at this moment; it is there, lifted up, dead, nailed to a post, and it has no more power over me. The cause of my deadly sickness has been taken away, lifted up in death, and it need never afflict me again." So life and health and peace would flow through the body of the sick man; he would look and live.

It dawned on me the other day, and with this thought came a much clearer understanding of the truth of Romans 6, that God told Moses to make a brazen serpent, one that was unquestionably dead. He did not tell him to take a living, fiery serpent and nail it to the post, and let it writhe and lash its tail, and struggle to live. The sight that would bring peace and healing was the dead serpent. It was a brazen serpent, and brass in the Bible speaks of judgment—God's judgment and my judgment passed irrevocably and finally upon the sin that is spoiling my life. We have agreed to pass a death sentence, and the death sentence has been carried out.

"Crucified with Christ, that the body of sin might be destroyed," but crucifixion is a long and painful process, a lingering, agonizing death, from the moment the condemned man stretches out his hands to be nailed, to the moment when he draws his last breath, and it is the same with my crucified self. There comes a moment when I yield mentally to the crucifixion of my old self with Christ and accept the principles of Christian life, after which there may ensue, perhaps must ensue, a period of tortured, struggling life. We will not come down from the Cross; we seek the lowest place, we give up our rights; we accept slights meekly; we deny ourselves, but our spirits are worn out, and we are on the verge of breakdown. We are consumed by our hurt pride, our struggling jealousy, our wounded self-love; at first they struggle to live; at last they are weary to die. We suffer far more than the natural, uncrucified man, who is free to use his own limbs for his own purposes, and to plan and scheme for his own advancement. The natural man stands by, and views with scorn, and some amusement, the heartaches and struggles of the Christian committed to the crucified life.

What is the point of it all? Probably, that before we can hate ourselves enough to jettison ourselves to death, we must know ourselves as we truly are. This crucifixion brings out the very worst in us; there is no veneer of respectability or hypocrisy left on the crucified man. "We receive the due reward of our deeds," cried the dying thief, facing himself for the first time. All the unguessed dregs and poisons of our conscious and subconscious minds, that have perhaps lain quiescent till now, will rise up in protest at such treatment, and cry out to live. Never before have we guessed the depths and strength of sin in our lives, until we yield them up to crucifixion. It is not the realization of what we must do that appalls us, but the realization of what we are; the coming to light of that life which struggles at all costs to life. There wasn't an evil passion that existed that had not been fully brought to light in that desert, from the moment when they set out on their journey, redeemed by the blood of the Lamb. The serpent was still writhing; struggling to live, weary to die.

"How long?" we cry. And there is no one answer to that. When we have fully seen and learned and accepted, the Lord says, "It is enough! I will give you rest; you shall die." And for some that time comes soon, and some struggle and agonize and strain all their lives. But this last is not God's will, for He purposed our peace, and the power of the new Resurrection life of Jesus which can only operate after the final death sentence has been passed and will only continue to operate as that sentence continues to be passed moment by moment.

Outward conflict there will always be; Israel's battles increased after this as they neared the border of the land, and the disciples suffered more after Pentecost than before, but their inward attitude was different. After Israel had looked at the serpent, we read no more of jealousy, or murmuring, or discouragement, or unbelief. Instead of battling with themselves, they could turn their attention to their outward enemies, the Moabites and the Amorites. Having dealt with the plague of their own heart, they could now start claiming territory for God.

They looked, and they lived. But first, in that desperate dying gaze, they died. It was as though God said to them, "It is enough; you shall die." The struggle, the tearing resentment, the poison of discontent shall cease. I have taken them out of the way, nailing them to My Cross. They have died in My Son. The Cross shall no longer be an instrument of torture, but the rest of your heart, the place where you bow your head, and give up the fight. The life you shall know now shall no longer be an agonizing, struggling, dying thing; it will be the very life of Jesus, surging up quietly from the depths of your being, like living waters, cleansing, strengthening, lifting up your head; only look and die; look and live."

And after that it was different. In verses 10-12 a new purpose came into life. Instead of wandering round in circles, they suddenly found their direction. They journeyed toward the sunrising with the light of a new dawning day ever before them. Instead of looking round and back, they looked forward and up. In verses 15-18, there was a new uprising of praise; even down in the hot, thirsty valley there was singing instead of complaining; and then, or course, the wells of God's grace sprang up, and they did not thirst any more, for God always works in response to praise and thanksgiving in trial. Murmuring and criticizing had been taken out of the way, nailed to His cross.

There was a new separation and single-mindedness too. They were passing through an alien land. "We will not turn into the fields or into the vineyards," they said. "We will not drink of the waters of the well. But we will go along by the King's highway, until we be past thy borders." They had actually said this before, but with what longing and discontent they would have lingered near those green oases. Now they were satisfied with God's manna, and they felt no desire for the luscious fruits and wells of the Amorites. They preferred to go straight on; those worldly lusts had been lifted up, nailed to the cross.

Lastly, there was a new power. With that inner conflict resolved, they could throw every ounce into the conflict round about them; there was a new peace and a new warfare, and they were victorious every time. Their journey was a pageant of victory. They had to fight for every foothold; they were often weary, sometimes wounded, perhaps afraid; but oh, the joy of it! The strongholds were falling, and the enemy was giving way, and it will always be so, because the great enemy was conquered once for all, and his stronghold routed, when the Lord was crucified, and the serpent was lifted up.

A short time ago I read of a Chinese Christian, slowly dying of an incurable, painful disease. He wrote the following lines which seem to epitomize the chapter:

With Him, with Him upon the tree,
My fear and grief have died;
I look in vain for misery,
And joy is all that I can see,
With Jesus crucified.

Strong pain has held me in its sway
For six long, weary years,
And yet my heart is always gay,
My lips are singing all the day,
I have no time for tears.